Pokemon

Yippee Yippee

Pikachu

1

2

3

Pikachu

4

5

6

Meowth

1

2

3

Meowth

6

5

4

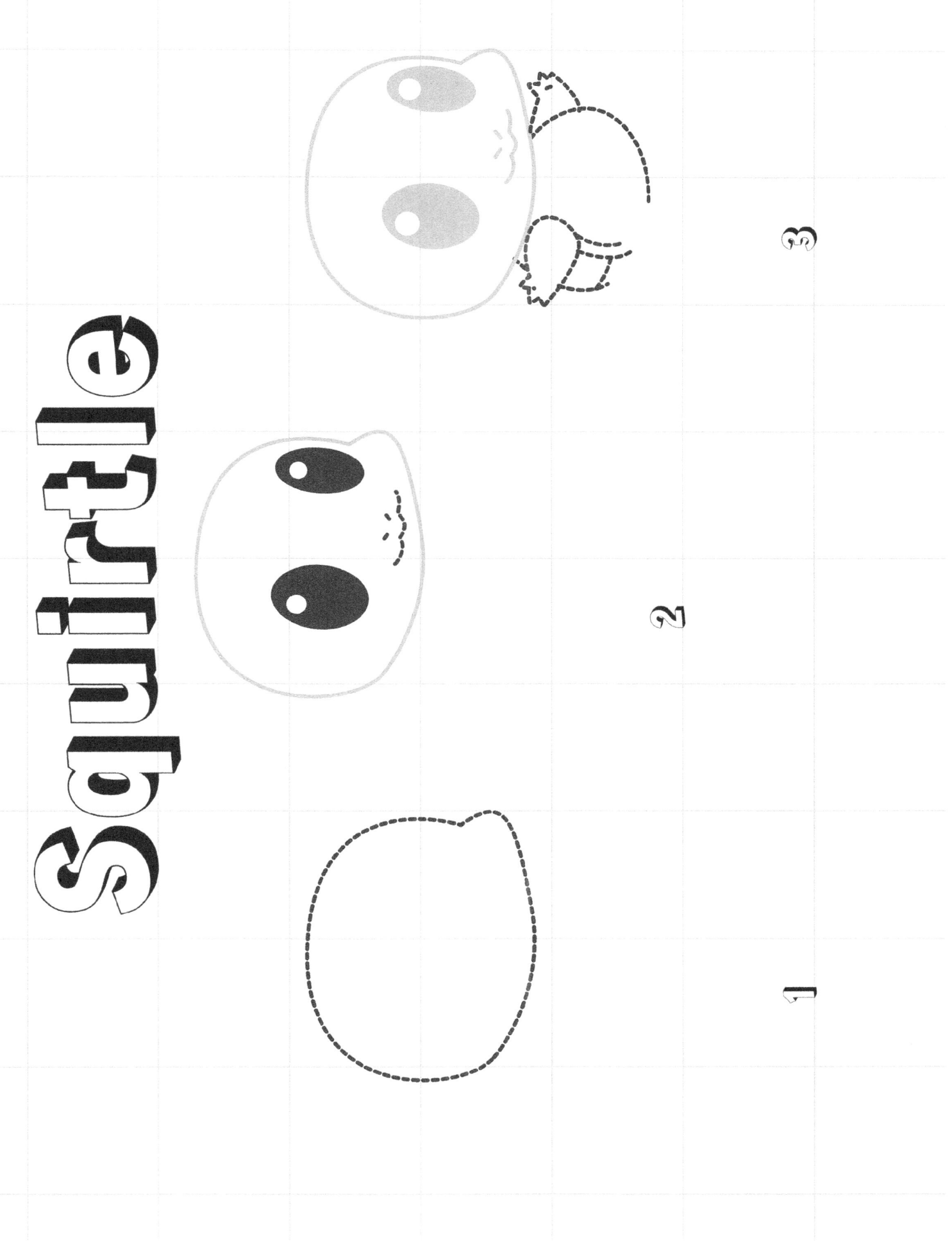

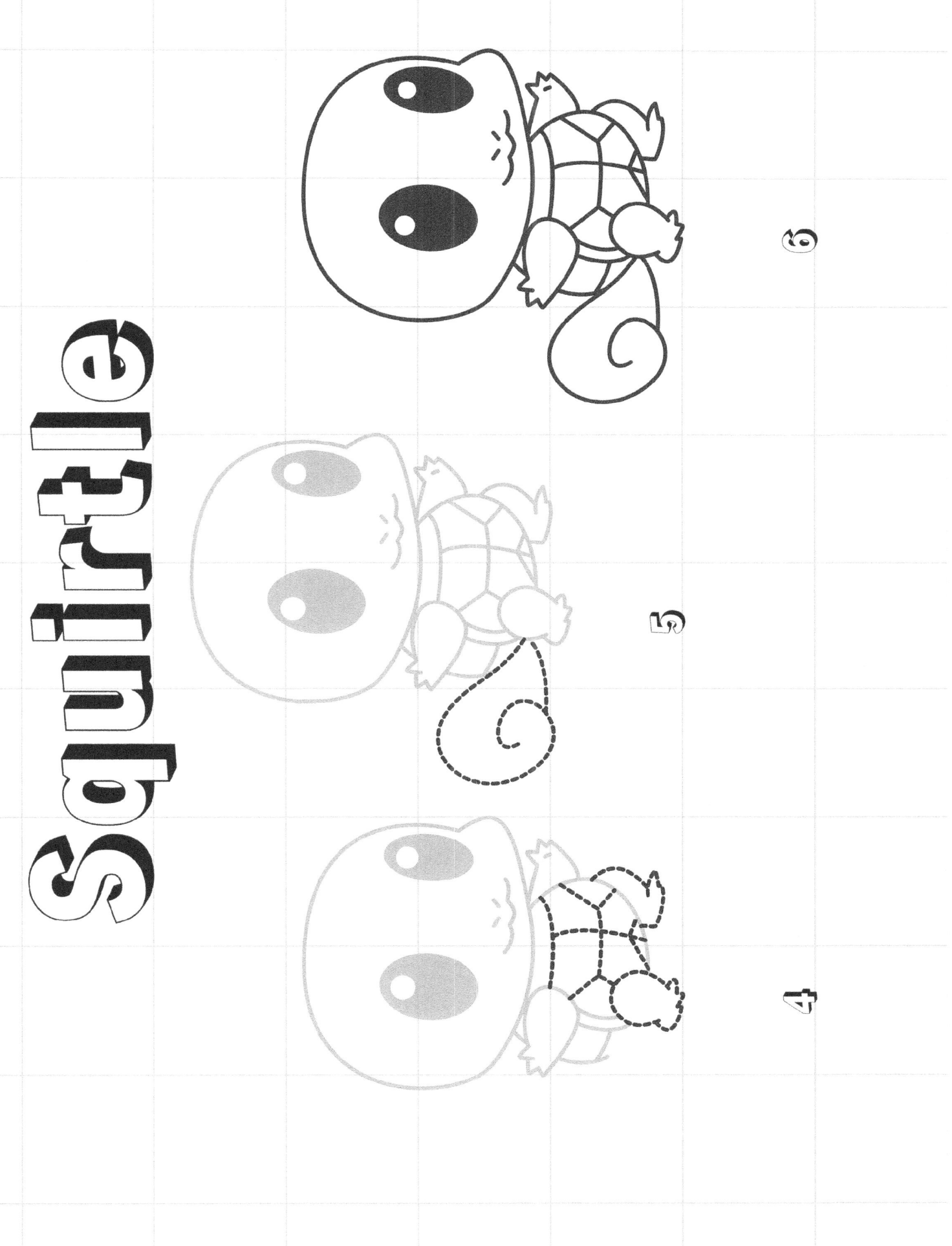

Bulbasaur

1

2

3

Bulbasaur

6

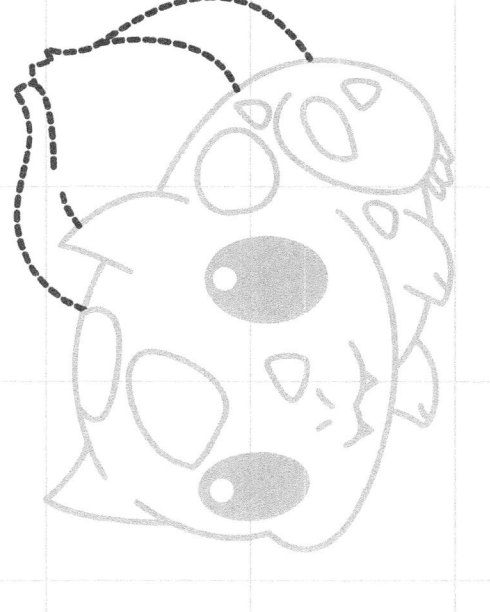

5

4

Snorlax

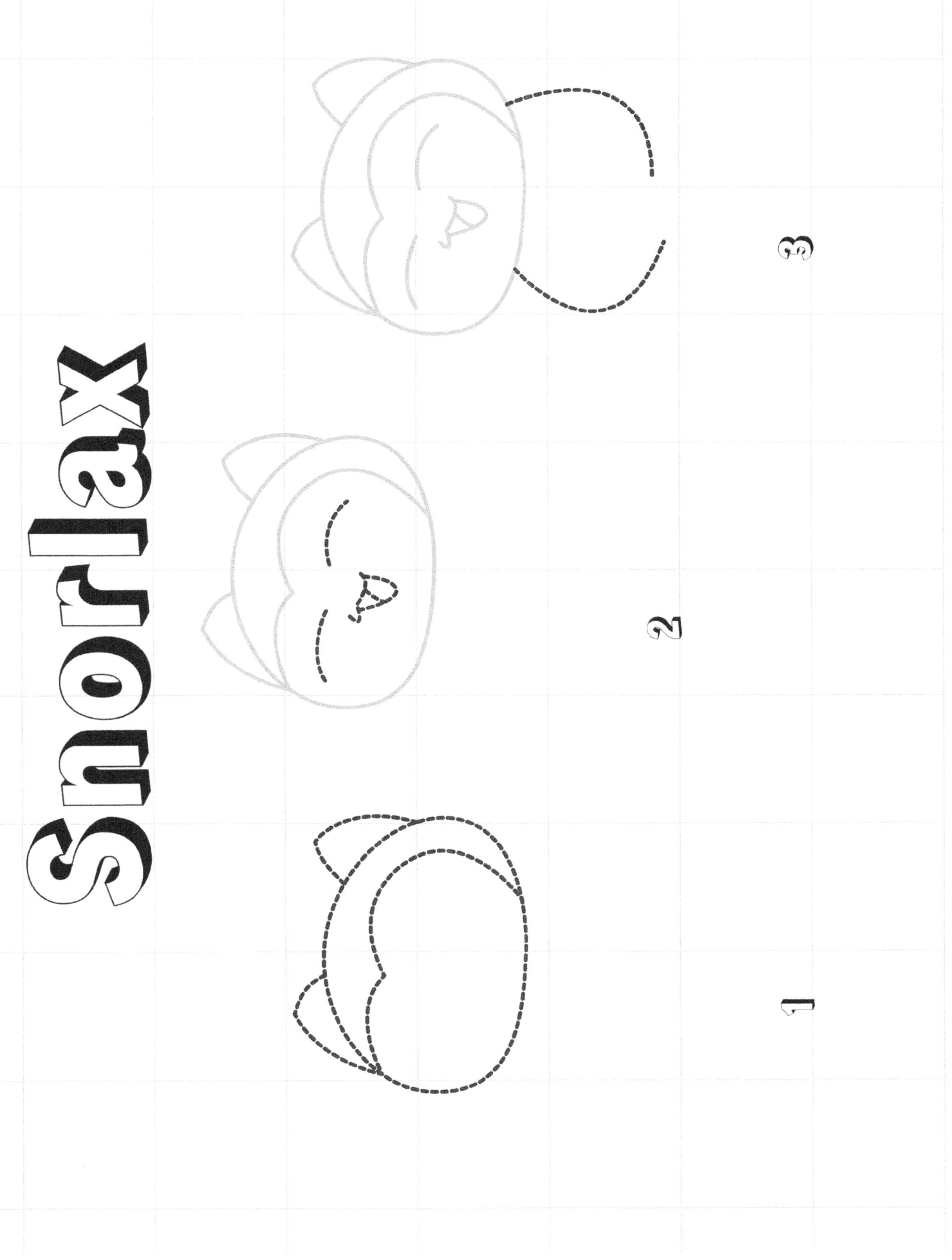

Snorlax

6

5

4

Cubone

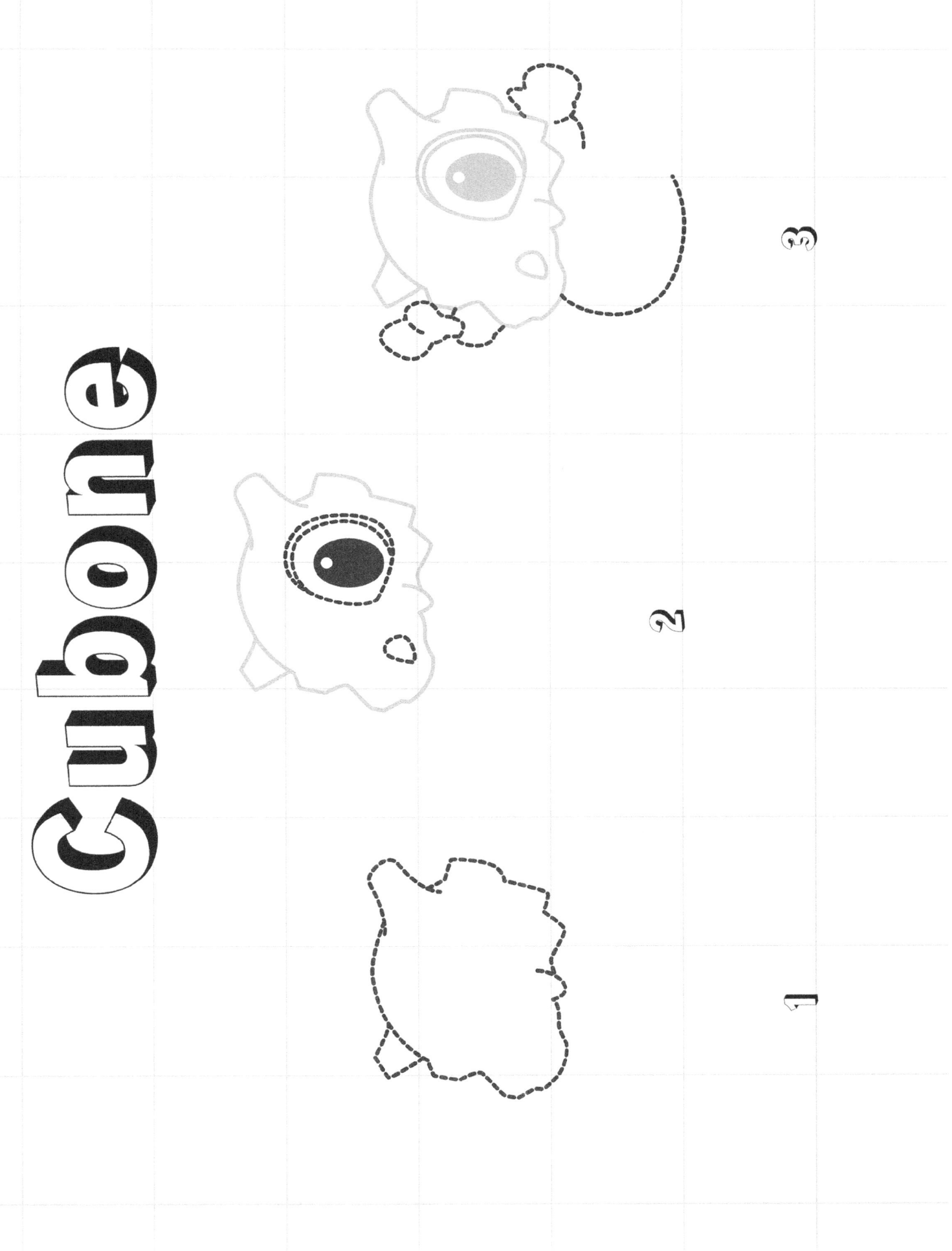

1

2

3

Cubone

6

5

4

Charmander

1

2

3

Charmander

6

5

4

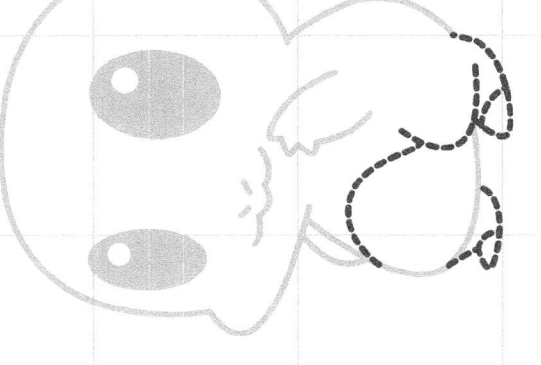

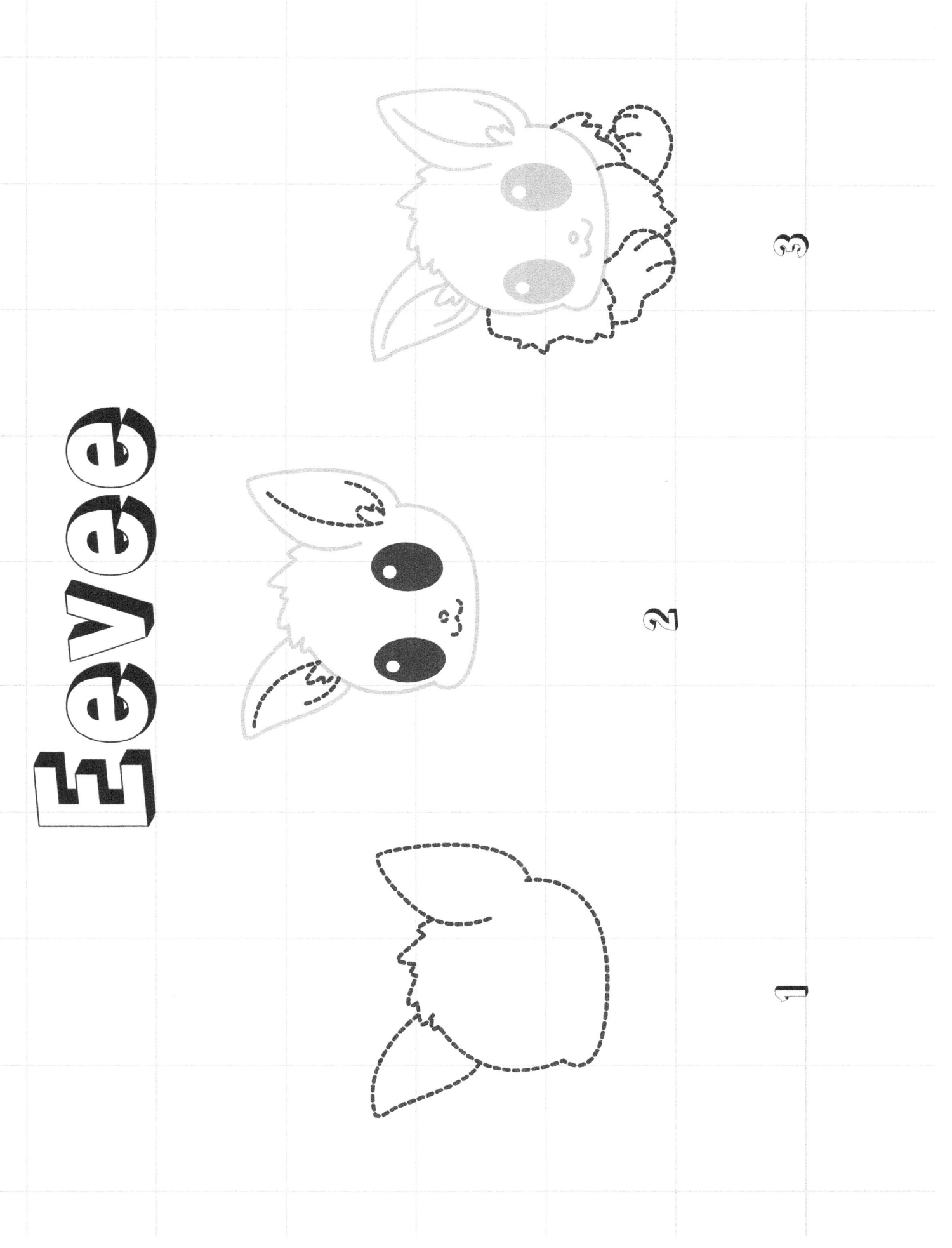

Eevee

1

2

3

Jigglypuff

1

2

3

Jigglypuff

6

5

4

Spheal

1

2

3

Spheal

3

5

4

Grookey

1

2

3

Grookey

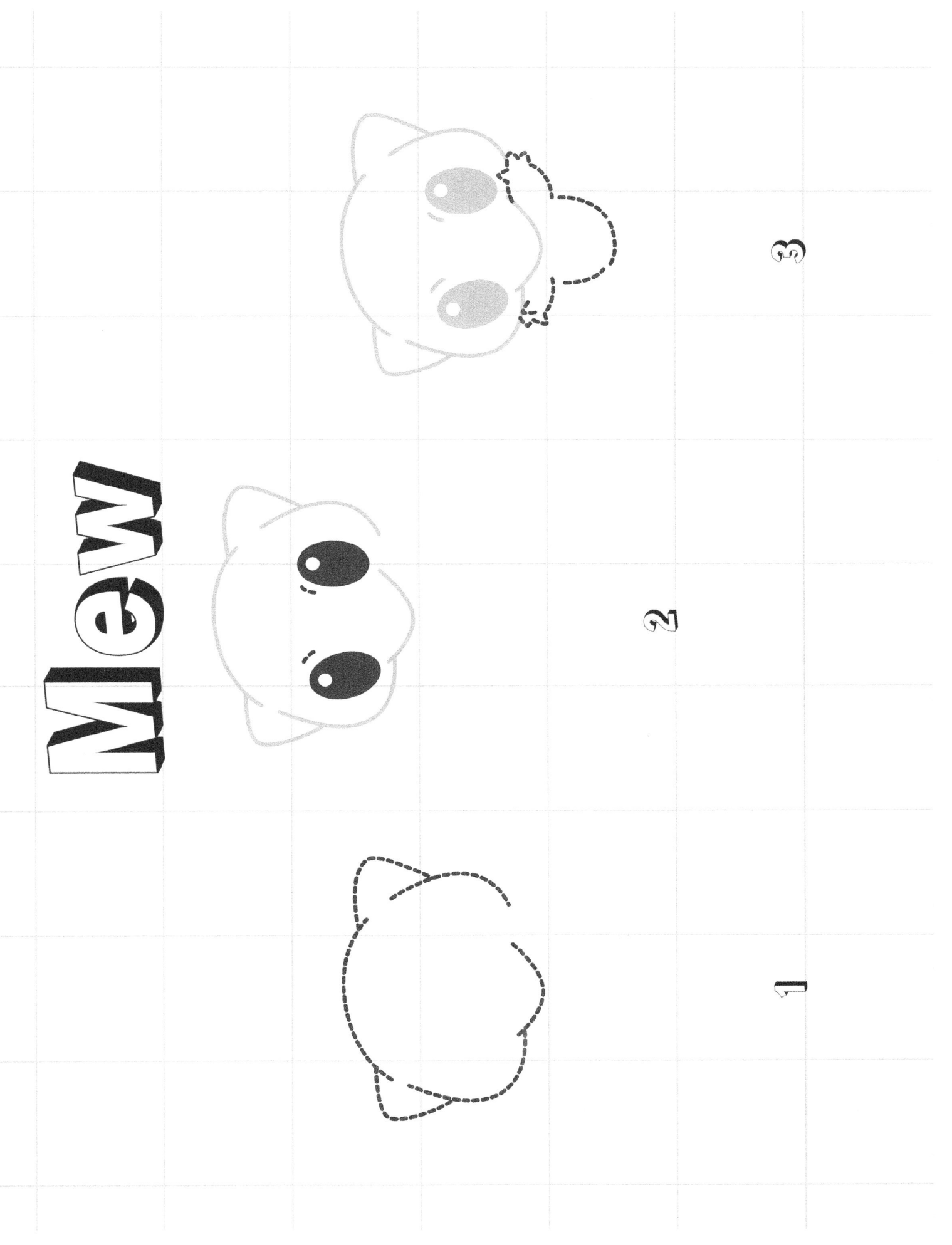

Togedemaru

1

2

3

Togedemaru

6

5

4

Minccino

1

2

3

Minccino

6

5

4

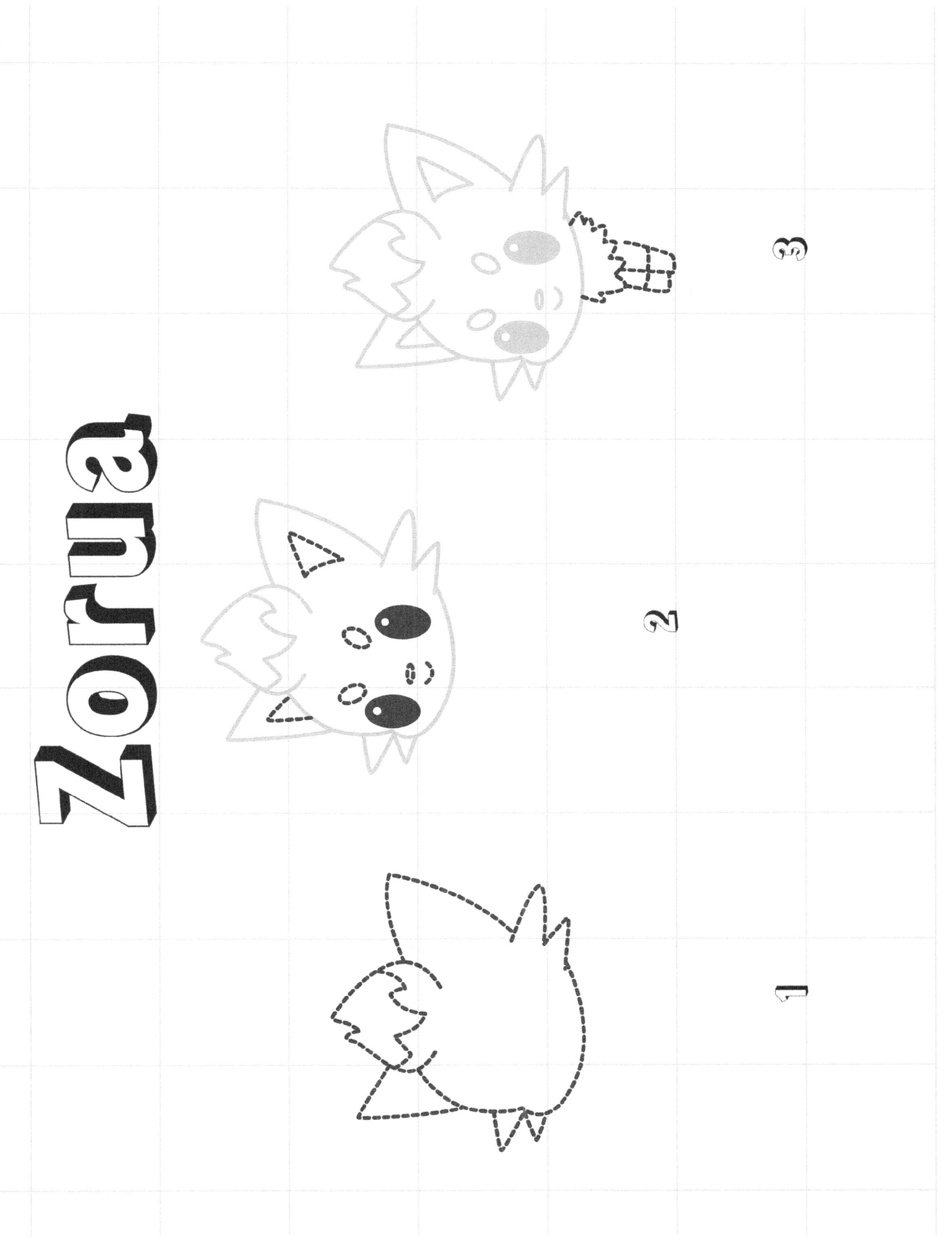

Zorua

Zorua

6

5

4

Togepi

Treecko

1

2

3

Treeecko

6

5

4

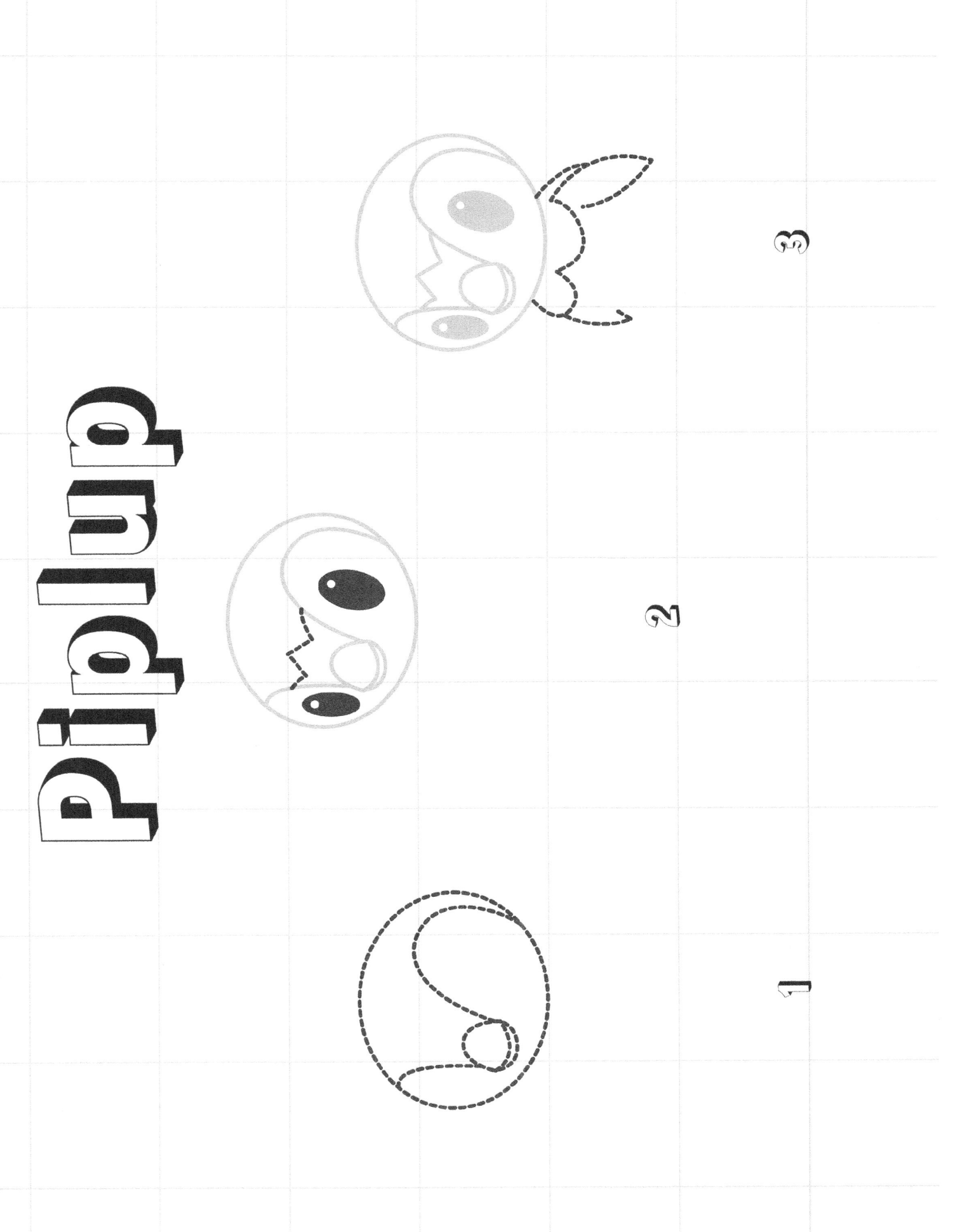

Piplup

1

2

3

Piplup

4

5

6

Pancham

1

2

3

Pancham

4

5

6

Sandslash

1

2

3

Sandslash

4

5

6

Vulpix

1

2

3

Vulpix

5

4

Mudkip

1

2

3

Mudkip

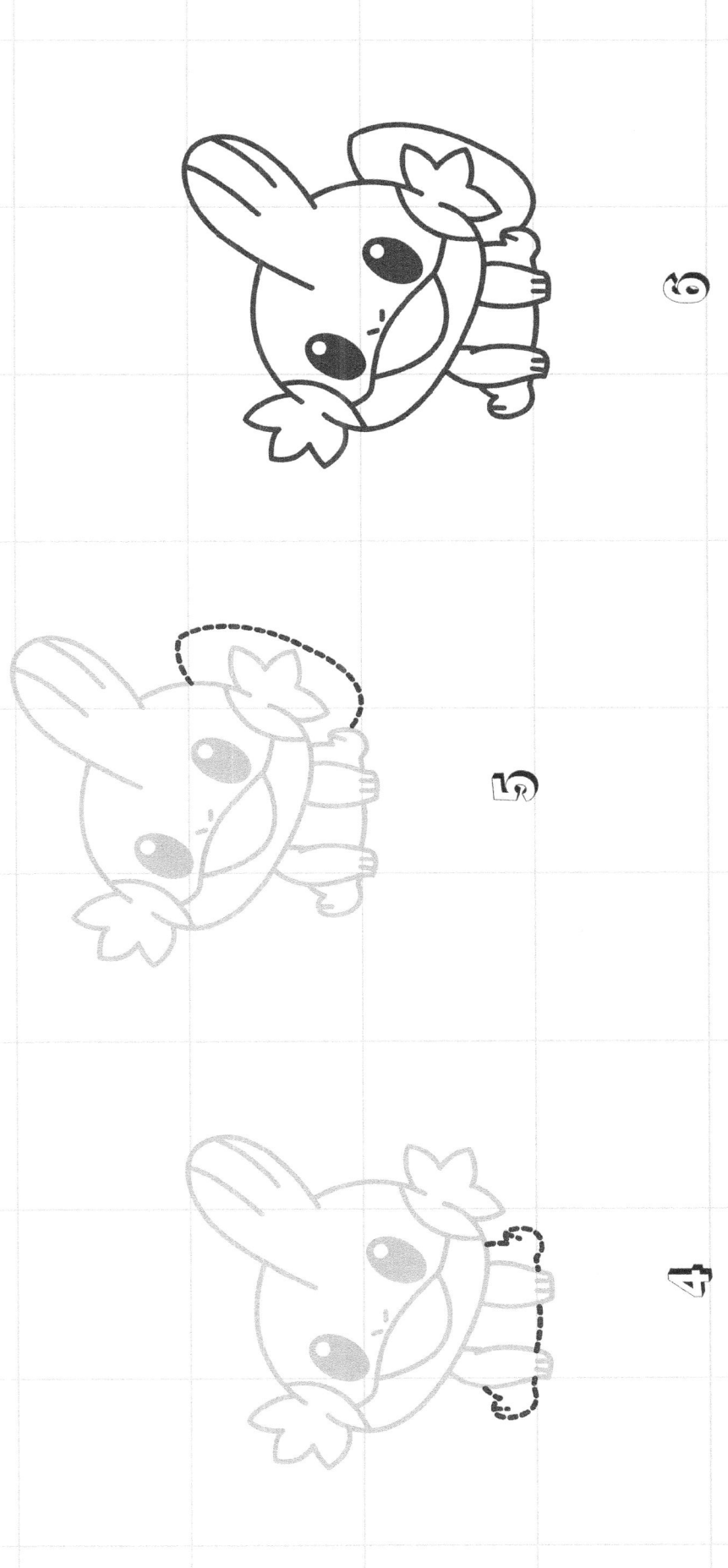

4

5

6

Torchic

1

2

3

Torchic

6

5

4

Vaporeon

1

2

3

Vaporeon

6

5

4

Umbreon

1

2

3

Umbreon

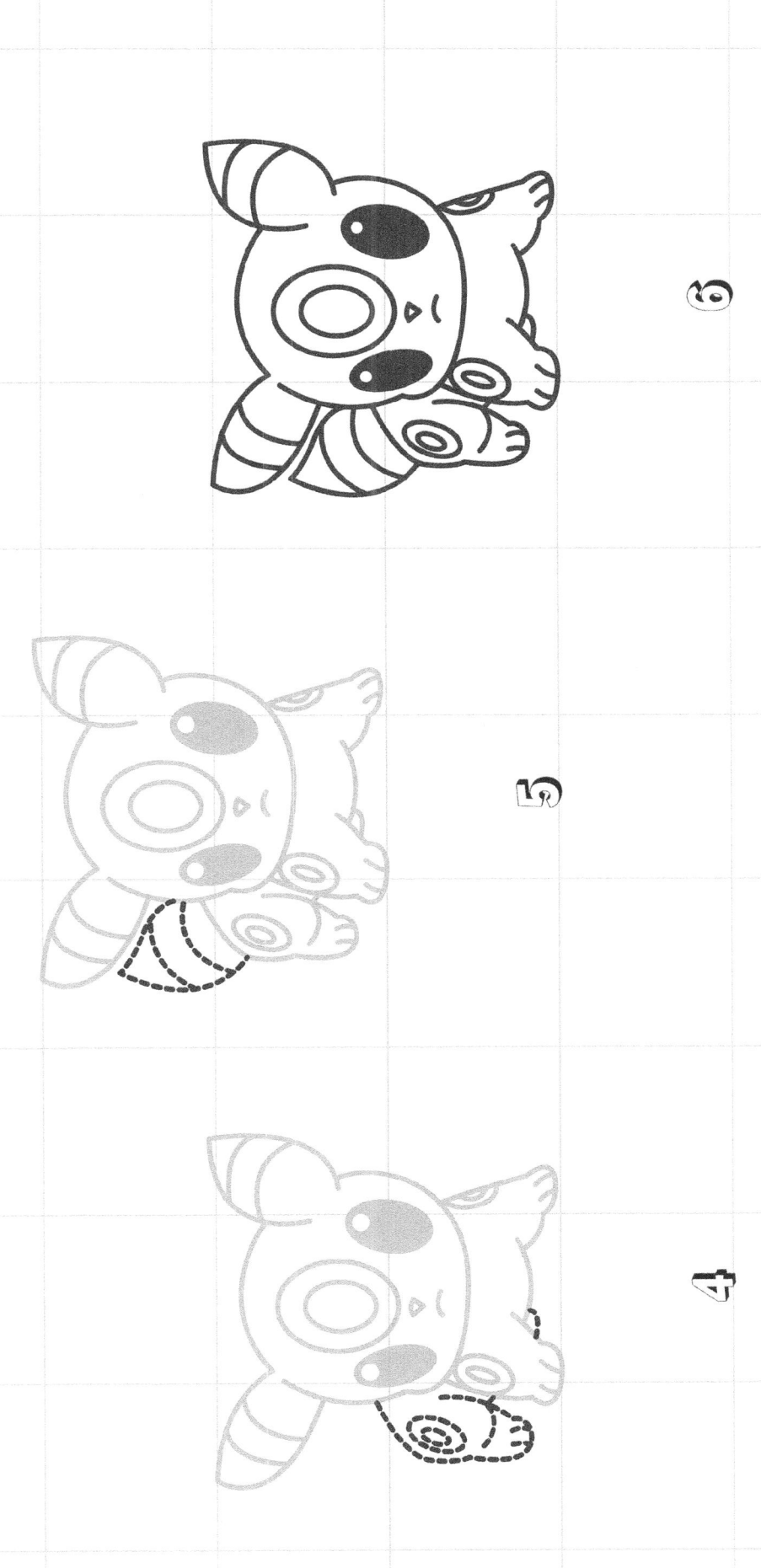

4

5

6

Made in the USA
Monee, IL
05 April 2022

94168332R00057